To Simon Christmas 1988. The Kings

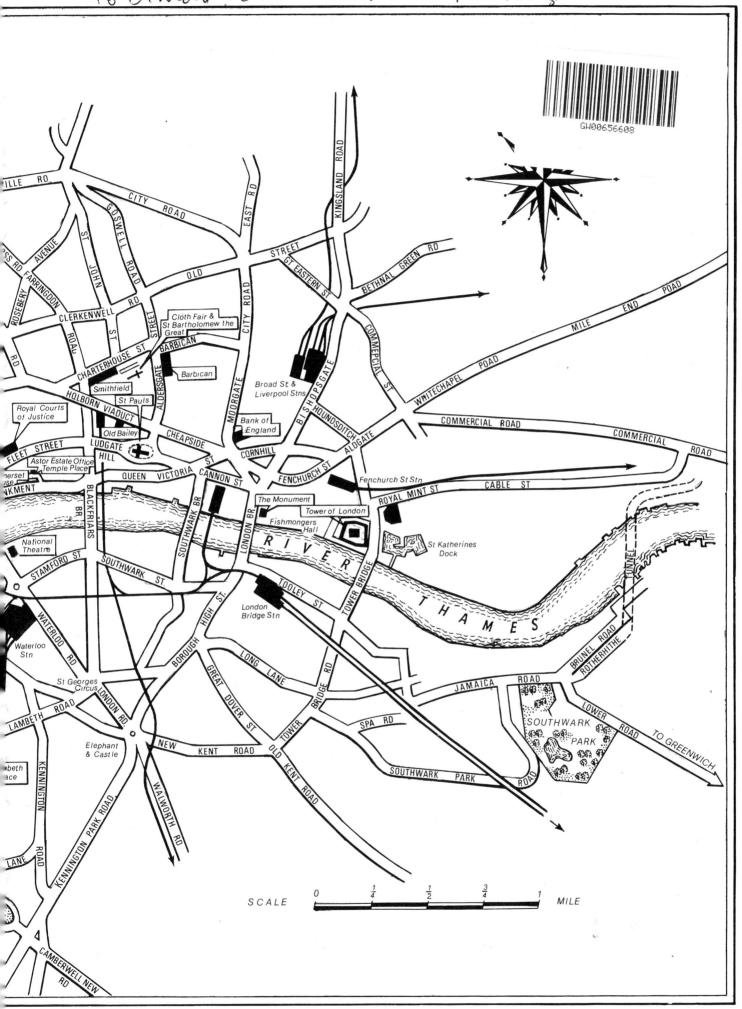

England in cameracolour
London

England in cameracolour
London

Photographs by: ANDY WILLIAMS
Text by: FRANCESCA BARRAN

Earth has not anything to show more fair,
Dull would he be of soul who could pass by
A sight so touching in its majesty:
This City now doth, like a garment wear
The beauty of the morning; silent, bare
Ships, towers, domes, theatres, and temples lie
Open unto the fields and to the sky
All bright and glittering in the smokeless air

Composed upon Westminster Bridge 1807
William Wordsworth

Town
County
BOOKS

LONDON

Bibliography

The Penguin Guide to London; F. R. Banks, Allen Lane, 1977
The Buildings of England: London (Cities of London and Westminster); Nikolaus Pevsner, Penguin Books
The King's England: London; Arthur Mee, Hodder & Stoughton, 1947
The Buildings of Britain; Alastair Service (series editor), Barrie & Watkins
   Anglo Saxon & Norman; Alastair Service, 1982
   Stuart and Baroque; Richard Morrice, 1982
   Regency; David Walker, 1982
Highways & Byways in London; Mrs E. T. Cook, 1907
London Growing; Michael Harrison, 1965
'Country Life' passim

First published 1983

ISBN 0 86364 007 9

Photographs © Andy Williams 1983

© Town & County Books Ltd 1983

Published by Town & County Books Ltd, Shepperton, Surrey;
and printed by Ian Allan Printing
at their works at Coombelands, Runnymede, England
Graphic reproduction by Southern Litho Services, Chertsey, Surrey.

Introduction

The earliest recorded mention of London is as the site of Queen Boadicea's famous defeat of the Romans in AD 61, but there must surely have been a pre-Roman settlement. Archaeological finds in the mud of the Thames indicate the existence of Celtic habitation and the etymology of the name reinforces the evidence. London is not a Roman name, it is derived from the Celtic god Lud or Lug, god of light, protector of waterways. Celtic London must have been centred round the twin defensible hills of Cornhill and Ludgate Hill with their protective streams of the Walbrook and the Fleet rivers, both now underground. There was also a ford at Billingsgate on which several pre-Roman roads converged.

For nearly four centuries the Romans ruled Britain from the imperial city of Londinium Augusta. They carried out punitive raids against the Celts and Picts and, at the beginning of the fourth century, under Constantine, they brought some peace to the province. But at the centre of the empire internecine wars demanded the return to Rome of the crack legions formerly stationed at the empire's outposts. In Britain as the military withdrew, the unruly tribesmen from the forests and Saxons from the sea began to harass the undefended Roman cities, making ever bolder attacks. It was in these uncertain times that London was first walled and, as far as is known, that wall remained impregnable for the next 600 years.

After the final retreat of the Romans there is no evidence of a sack of London. It seems probable therefore that the trading importance of the city was respected by the warring men of Kent and Wessex and neither side attempted to seize it. The next two centuries saw London in decline, and it reached its nadir at the time of the Danish invasion. In 874 AD the city was taken, from the river, by the Danes, but they did not occupy it, preferring to camp outside its walls to the west and south of the river — Southwark is a Danish name. In 878 AD they were defeated by Alfred the Great and the subsequent treaty confined their sphere of influence to East Anglia, Essex and part of Midland Mercia.

William of Normandy who came in 1066 was a different sort of invader. He wanted to be king, and he intended to be crowned in London, to assure his authority throughout the land with London as its capital. William was duly crowned in Edward the Confessor's Westminster Abbey, and London was forced to submit. William built the White Tower on the very walls of London in 1078 to ensure the continued good behaviour of its citizens. The city lands were not only parcelled up and divided amongst the Norman camp-followers, but also amongst the bishops and monastic orders who swarmed in behind them. The number and size of these establishments grew throughout the 13th century, until, by the end of that century, almost half the city's enclosed land was under some form of religious jurisdiction. The dissolution of the monasteries by King Henry VIII in 1538 stemmed more from motives of xenophobia and economic greed than from religion. Nevertheless, it was undoubtedly a source of satisfaction to the burghers of the city of London, and the place of the departing monks and nuns was quickly filled by merchants and traders of all kinds.

The 16th century also saw the first introduction of finance as opposed to mere trade into the activities of the City. London had its own bourse, modelled on that of Antwerp, opened in 1566 through the efforts of Britain's first recognised economist, Sir Thomas Gresham. The growing nationalism which had encouraged the English cheerfully to turn out the foreign religious orders at the Dissolution paradoxically also ensured that they welcomed the foreign opponents of the Roman Church. The end of the 16th century saw an enormous influx of Protestants from France, Germany, Holland and Flanders, all fleeing persecution in their own countries. Many of them — like the French Huguenot silk weavers of Spitalfields — brought specialist skills and set up ghettos where they lived and worked.

This too was the age of expansion of sea trade and the great voyages of discovery. Tremendous growth of docks and shipbuilding yards was necessary to provide the ships for these ventures. Greenwich, the country palace of Henry VII and Henry VIII was soon joined to the city by ribbon development along the river.

The first attempt to control the spread of London was made by Elizabeth I. A proclamation of 1580 declared that no new building within three miles of the walls of London would be allowed without licence. Another of the conditions for the granting of a licence by James I was that houses should be fronted wholly in brick, or brick and stone, that the street fronts should represent a uniform appearance, and furthermore that the upper storeys should not project above the lower. Sadly, these ordinances must have been completely disregarded for houses like that in Cloth Fair (plate 43) with its wooden oriels post-date the instructions and buildings like it must have contributed to the spread of the Fire of London when it came in 1666. James I's ambition for the regularisation of London streets was in part realised by his son Charles I. Inigo Jones' Covent Garden (plate 33) and Whitehall Banqueting House 5 (plate 19) became the ideal for both domestic and official building in the future. These small beginnings were halted by the Civil War, but on Charles II's restoration, the Italianate Classical style so closely associated with his martyred father, was the only acceptable style for subjects seeking Royal favour.

Two major forces led to the westward development of the city after the Restoration. First there was the desire by the land-owning aristocracy, or anyone with the resources to acquire leases, to develop Crown Land, to speculate in land development in London in emulation of the highly successful development of Covent Garden by the Duke of Bedford's Estate. At the same time tenants were provided by the westward migration of all who could afford to move upwind of the noxious airs of the old city which, it was believed, carried the plague. The earliest developments were Bloomsbury Square and St James's Square and their surrounding network of streets and others followed. Many aristocratic speculators, like Sir Thomas Bond and Sir Thomas Clarges, inevitably gave their names to the streets they developed.

When the Fire of London struck, it was viewed by many not directly affected as a Heaven-sent blessing. It not only purified the air and rid London of the previous year's plague but it also provided an opportunity to rebuild the city in the newly-accepted Classical mode with wide thoroughfares crossing at right angles and opening to wide squares and piazzas. While Sir Christopher Wren (d. 1732), the Church hierarchy, the City fathers, and the king bickered over the plans to rebuild St Paul's, the city shopkeepers and merchants speedily rebuilt what they had lost, more anxious to get on with business than to 'improve' London. Despite planning shortcomings it was a more beautiful London, safer, sweeter and more commodious.

Meanwhile the West End was growing apace. The land between the Temple and Charing Cross was developed by Nicholas Barbon (d. 1698), and here the street names recall George, Duke of Buckingham, over the site of whose riverside house and garden the streets rose (George Alley, Villiers Street, Duke Street, Ot Alley and Buckingham Street).

An important building Act of Parliament in the reign of Queen Anne (1702-1714) greatly changed the face of the mid-17th century developments. All London was still intensely anxious about the risk of fire and the Act recognised the great danger inherent in the quantity of exterior wood used in facades. Roofs were to be placed behind brick parapets and no longer carried on the deeply projecting wooden eaves supported by carved brackets, windows were to be recessed at least four inches, and the new Dutch-design sash windows used in preference to casement windows.

One of the first acts of the newly-elected high church Tory government under Queen Anne was to set up a Commission to order the building of 50 new churches in districts as far apart as Gravesend and Islington. The building of the Commission churches clearly marked the outlying suburbs as destined for eventual merger into a greater London. They were placed mainly east of the city in Wapping, Woolwich and Deptford but an equally far flung westward expansion was already ensured by William III's purchase of Nottingham House in 1689 as a London residence and subsequently Queen Anne's decision to make the newly-built Kensington Palace her permanent home. The Court needed lodgings nearby during their attendance on the queen and a speculative builder called Young built the complex of streets around Kensington Square.

The next major stage in the development of London came with the need for good quality roads to link the capital speedily and safely with the emerging industrial towns further north. Two bridges — Westminster and Blackfriar's — were built across the Thames, the first since the 12th century. The building of the new roads also ended the isolation of the villages around London and soon ribbon development linked Chelsea, Kensington, Islington and Hampstead to the north and Camberwell, Peckham, Newington, Vauxhall and Kennington to the south.

The end of the 18th century saw the birth of the collaboration between George, Prince of Wales, and John Nash (d. 1835), a corrupt but effective speculative builder. Thus for only the second time in London's history was there a ruler with both the taste and the will to exert it upon the improvement of the city. First came the replanning of central London from St James's Park to Regents Park through Regent Street and Portland Place which was completed by 1830. Particularly influential for future building design were the charming Italianate and neo-Tudor villas of Nash's Park Village East and West. These detached villas — not one resembles another — were the prototypes of the myriad of detached houses built all around London and other cities in the following century.

At the end of the 18th century and the beginning of the 19th there was a rapid expansion of trade as the British Empire steadily grew. The Napoleonic wars encouraged the concentration of mercantile and commercial activity in London and the ever increasing demand for shipping called for a development of the port of London and its ancillary services. In the first quarter of the 19th century five new docks were built — West India Dock on the Isle of Dogs, London Dock at Wapping, the Surrey Docks, the East India Dock and St Katherine's Dock. The soil excavated from the last of these was transported up river for the foundations of South Westminster, the Pimlico development by Thomas Cubitt. The East End too was developed with pretty little terraces of town houses for the clerks and managers who ran the docks, alongside the slums which are so integral a part of any shifting dockside population.

George IV's move from Carlton House to Buckingham Palace in 1827, turned the attentions of speculative builders to the development potential of the slums and marshes of Pimlico and Belgravia. Thomas Cubitt was a building contractor in the grand mould of Barbon and Nash. He had already been at work in Bloomsbury where he had built Gordon Square and Woburn Place. The Earl of Grosvenor's Estate which owned the land had bided its time for nearly a century, but here saw the green light to develop. Belgrave Square, Eaton Square, Lowndes Square and Eaton Place as well as many of the interconnecting streets all came from Cubitt's drawing office between 1825 and 1873. Surprisingly, all this outward expansion of London was going on when the clerks and workmen who lived in it still commuted on foot. Even the arrival of the horsedrawn omnibus in 1829 did little to alter this pattern. It was not until the coming of the railways that the outlying suburbs could also be developed.

By 1860 most of Surrey and North Kent had been linked to the capital by rail and the outward spread of London's boundaries steadily gathered pace. People and industry were steadily withdrawing from the centre of the city in search of fresher air and cheaper land. But building on a considerable scale continued until well into the 20th century. In Camberwell, for example, some 416 builders built 5,760 houses in the years 1878-80. The Edwardian era saw some London building but the 'dream houses' of the era for all classes were well out of the city. The trend continued through the inter-war period, growing steadily in momentum. Then came World War 2 with a devastation of the City in 1940-41 even worse than that of the Great Fire in 1666 — to say nothing of the acres of houses destroyed in the docklands area of the East End and the extensive destruction of houses in the suburbs. The postwar solution — green belt restrictions and new 'satellite' towns that uprooted thousands; the destruction of sound terraced houses on the grounds of 'slum clearance' and their replacement with high rise flats, was at best only partially successful, lacking as it did the essentially human dimension of earlier developments.

Just as the last acres of development land were being gobbled up the pattern changed. Outer suburbia, in what has become known as the 'Home Counties', began to attract ever increasing numbers of immigrants from London. Soon the offices and factories were following them tempted by cheaper rents and rates. It was a tendency that continued until well after World War 2. Governments encouraged the flow by the planning of new towns like Bracknell, Crawley and Milton Keynes, offering grants as an additional incentive to removal from London. The 1960s and 1970s saw an enormous drop in the population of Central London. More recently however the outward trend seems to be reversing. Government is striving to stem inner city decay and to entice factories, offices and people back into the former docklands area — a prospect more attractive now than it has been for centuries. London may no longer be the largest or the most powerful capital in the world. As a place to live it is now undoubtedly one of the most civilised. It bids fair to be the world's leading centre for music and the arts and as the pages which follow amply demonstrate, it boasts an architectural heritage which few other cities can rival.

Francesca Barran
LONDON, 1983

Hampton Court Palace, Kingston upon Thames. Originally Hampton Court was Cardinal Wolsey's creation. On it he expended his considerable fortune and great artistic acumen. He imported Italians to work on it and thereby was responsible for the earliest introduction of Renaissance architecture into English domestic building. On his fall from grace to which it in no small way contributed, Hampton Court became a favourite residence of Henry VIII (1509-47) and has remained royal property ever since. The next great additions were on the accession of William of Orange and Mary in 1689. The house they commissioned Sir Christopher Wren to build on to the old Tudor palace was a comfortable country house in red brick with stone dressing, evoking happy memories of The Hague. The gardens followed the French mode of Le Notre with great avenues, formal waters and statues. Many of the same distinguished artists who had collaborated with Wren on St Paul's Cathedral and his city churches, worked on Hampton Court as well. The wonderfully intricate ironwork balustrades on the staircases and the garden gates are the work of Jean Tijou while Grinling Gibbons provided carved panels and chimney pieces for the king's suite of rooms. Of Wolsey's and Henry's Palace the great hall, kitchen and Wolsey's cabinet still remain.

The Palace and gardens, including the famous maze are open daily.

8

Parliament Square, Westminster. This statue of Sir Winston Churchill (d. 1965) stands on the green in Parliament Square appropriately facing the House of Commons which Sir Winston loved and embellished with his wisdom and wit for so long. The statue is by Ivor Roberts-Jones and was completed in 1973. Sir Winston's statue shares the grassy centre of the Square with several illustrious predecessors — Lord Palmerston (d. 1865); Benjamin Disraeli, Lord Beaconsfield (d. 1881); Sir Robert Peel (d. 1850); and Lord Canning (d. 1827). Other statues in the Square are of Field Marshal Smuts (d. 1950) and Abraham Lincoln (d. 1865).

The Clock Tower of the Houses of Parliament holds the great bell (over $13\frac{1}{2}$ tons) known as 'Big Ben' whose sound is familiar all over the world. It takes its name from Sir Benjamin Hall who was Commissioner of Works in 1858 when the bell was cast.

Albert Bridge, Chelsea. A combined
cantilever and suspension bridge built in
1873 by R. W. Ordish, the Albert Bridge
links Battersea on the south with Chelsea
on the north bank of the Thames. At night
gaily decked out with lights it looks like a
great liner dressed overall, and is perhaps
the prettiest of all London's bridges. Just
beyond it can be seen the great chimneys of
Lots Road power station. The Chelsea
Embankment was constructed in 1871 and
houses were promptly built all along it, to
take advantage of the fine views over the
river. This is one of the pleasantest
stretches of river in London, the intimate
nature of the buildings makes an agreeable
distraction and the trees of Battersea Park
on the further side of the river form a pretty
12   backdrop at all seasons of the year.

The Royal Hospital, Chelsea. This is one of those rare instances of a charitable foundation still fulfilling its original purpose after 300 years. By the mid-17th century the principle of providing a home for old and wounded soldiers had been generally accepted. Louis XIV built Les Invalides in Paris and Charles II felt that he could do no less and commissioned Sir Christopher Wren to produce plans. The buildings form a three-sided court, the side towards the river remaining open, more like a palace in design than a hospital. Inside there were even more innovations such as the long corridors linking the wards in the side blocks which house some 300 pensioners. The Hall and Chapel flank the central entrance of the main block behind the low colonnade and are lit from above by tall round-headed windows. Originally there were elaborate formal gardens leading to the river but these were swept away to be replaced by lawns which, for a week at the end of May each year, are the site of the world-renowned Chelsea Flower Show.

The guns on display here include a battery captured at Waterloo.

The Albert Memorial, Kensington Gardens.
This was the site of the Great Exhibition of 1851, which was the brain-child of Prince Albert, the Prince Consort, and possibly his greatest contribution to the realm. Here, beneath Paxton's great glass dome, were erected stands from the four corners of the world exhibiting products of every kind and size. For Britain the mid-19th century was the high point of the development of the manufacturing industries, British colonies stretched from China to the West Indies and from Australia to Africa and India was the jewel in the diadem. It is fitting therefore that Queen Victoria should have erected on this site the memorial to her beloved husband. (The original proposal to place the monument on top of the Albert Hall, which it faces, was, happily, abandoned.)

At each corner of the Memorial stand representations of the Four Continents and similar groups symbolising Agriculture, Manufacture, Commerce and Engineering. Around the base runs a frieze depicting all the great and good men of history. Above the statue of Prince Albert the gothic baldacchino rises on four pink columns, decorated with mosaics, statues and pinnacles. It was designed by one of the great architects of the day, Sir George Gilbert Scott (d. 1878) and it was erected in 1863-76.

16

The Albert Hall, Kensington. Built between 1867-71 and paid for in part by money left over from the public subscription raised for the erection of the Albert Memorial, the Albert Hall has little of the lush decoration of mosaics and statues which distinguish the Memorial. In fact it is, just a vast brick drum beneath a glass and iron dome. Its seating capacity of 8,000 ensured however that music could be brought to an ever-increasing concert-going public, and it has been, appropriately, since the 1939-45 war, the home of the world-famous Promenade concerts founded by Sir Henry Wood in 1895. Nowadays the Albert Hall is almost as well known as the venue for all-in wrestling and tennis tournaments, as it is for concerts or productions of Handel's *Messiah*. The management has contrived successfully to keep abreast of the times, by giving space in its programme to pop concerts and other happenings in between the Women's Institute, the Royal British Legion's, and the Salvation Army's annual gatherings — and

the Promenade season.

The Natural History Museum, Cromwell Road, Kensington. The profits from the Great Exhibition of 1851 were used at the express wish of the Prince Consort to buy 88 acres of land to provide a site for a cultural and educational centre. The first building to be constructed on the site was the so-called 'Brompton Boilers', which served as a first home for the Victoria and Albert Museum — it was pulled down and rebuilt in 1899-1909. The Natural History Museum, built between 1873-81, is the earliest surviving museum of the planned complex. It was built by Alfred Waterhouse in a romanesque style — characterised by its round arches. The casing material is terracotta slabs, a favourite material with the Victorians, appealing as it did to notions of cleanliness and economy — the slabs were intended to be self washing. As befits its purpose the exterior ornamentation is strictly zoological, animals and birds of every description perch and hang and spring from the most unlikely surfaces.

Inside the museum are halls and galleries devoted to an unrivalled collection of specimens from all parts of the world. One gallery contains remains of the dinosaurs, another skeletons of huge fish like the blue whale, others with small creatures like spiders and sea urchins.

Apsley House, Hyde Park Corner, Westminster. The original Apsley House was built in 1771-78 by Robert Adam for Henry Bathurst, Baron Apsley. It was smaller than the present house and brick-fronted. In 1817 the Duke of Wellington, freshly returned from the peace negotiations in the aftermath of the Napoleonic Wars, bought the house and in 1828 employed the architects Benjamin and Philip Wyatt to enlarge it, case it in stone and add the famous Waterloo Gallery. Here each year on the anniversary of the battle he gave a great banquet for veterans of his campaigns. The last house in Piccadilly, Apsley House for some time rejoiced in the address 'No 1, London'.

Having exchanged the role of successful general for that of prime minister, Wellington did not always enjoy the same popularity. On the night of 27 April 1831 a mob gathered outside the house to protest about his opposition to the Reform Bill. They hurled stones and managed to break several windows. The Duke's response was speedy and typical. He had iron shutters put up for use in any future emergency, swearing never again, in his own house, to be put at the mercy of an angry mob.

The house, which has recently been extensively redecorated, is now an outpost of the Victoria and Albert Museum. Many memorabilia of the Iron Duke are exhibited here including gifts made to him by the grateful people of Spain and Portugal, along with his considerable collection of Napoleonic souvenirs amongst which is an 11ft high nude heroic statue of Napoleon by the Italian sculptor Canova. Opposite the house (on the left of the photograph) is a bronze statue of the Duke riding his famous horse, Copenhagen, which carried him into battle at Waterloo. The horse lived on until 1836 to be buried, finally, with full military honours at Strathfield Saye, Wellington's country house in Hampshire.

Boodle's Club, St James's Street, Westminster. Boodle's Club, founded in 1762, was formed like so many others, out of a casual group who regularly took coffee or chocolate together at the same place and, being of like mind, set themselves up as a private club, more by accident of usage than by any well devised plan. Boodle's originally welcomed women as members, the principal entertainment was gambling and women played for as high stakes as men. The betting book is still retained amongst the Club's archives and records many outlandish bets. The club was also noted for some extravagant entertainments. A masquerade in 1774 cost no less than 2,000 guineas to put on.

Boodle's moved to its present building in 1765 and the elegant facade on St James's has a characteristic bay window to the morning room. Above is the venetian window of the saloon, one of the most elegant rooms in London, very much in the Adam style, though probably by an imitator.

The club has always tended to attract members of the landed gentry though it is a little hard to find any common denominator between former members in the past like Charles James Fox, who was noted for his drunken revels; Gibbon, the author of the *Decline and Fall of the Roman Empire*; and Wilberforce the great reformer and emancipator of the slaves.

24

Buckingham Palace, St James's, Westminster. The London residence of the kings and queens of England since 1762 when George III (1760-1820) bought it for his German Queen, Charlotte. It was originally built by the Duke of Buckingham in 1705 as a country residence on the edge of the city of Westminster. Indeed, something of the feeling of a country house is still there when one looks at the classical facade visible over the wall on Constitution Hill. Buckingham House, as it then was, soon proved to be too small for George III's growing family — he had 11 children — and he was virtually forced to move to Windsor. In 1824 George IV, the former Prince Regent, decided that Carlton House, built for him by Nash, on which he had spent many thousands, was 'Little better than a hovel' and he asked Nash to put Buckingham House in order. It then became Buckingham Palace. The east front seen here was reconstructed by Sir Aston Webb in 1913. At the centre of the principal floor is the famous balcony where, by tradition, the royal family appears on great public and national occasions, most recently after the wedding of the Prince and Princess of Wales.

Buckingham Palace is the principal seat of the Queen and whenever she is in residence the Royal Standard is flown.

In the centre of the open space in front of the Palace is the Queen Victoria Memorial in white marble surmounted by a gilt bronze figure of victory. The sculptor was Sir Thomas Brook and the monument was erected in 1911.

26

Lambeth Palace, Lambeth. This photograph shows the red brick Tudor entrance to Lambeth Palace, called Morton's Tower. The building on the right is St Mary's Church, the parish church of Lambeth, now disused. Lambeth Palace has been the London residence of the Archbishops of Canterbury for over 700 years. The name Lambeth means a muddy landing place — there was no bridge here until the 18th century and Horseferry road on the opposite bank is another survival from the pre-bridge days.

In the Middle Ages Lambeth was only one of 19 archepiscopal palaces dotted over Surrey, Sussex and Kent, but as the nearest to Westminster it was always the most important. (The Archbishop would progress, on his journeys between London and Canterbury, stopping a night at each house.) The oldest surviving building is the chapel, and the crypt below it dates from 1210, the upper part from a dozen years later. Archbishop Laud (1573-1645) remodelled the chapel during his occupancy and when he was charged with high treason in 1640, these works were among the other charges levelled against him during his trial. He was allowed to return to Lambeth, just once, to collect a book or two with which to while away the four years he was to spend incarcerated in the Tower of London awaiting execution. A portrait of him by Van Dyck still hangs in the Palace.

During the Commonwealth (1649-60) Lambeth Palace was used as a prison for royalists, among them the poet Sir Richard Lovelace who recalled his time there in the immortal lines *'Stone walls do not a prison make, Nor iron bars a cage'.*

At the Restoration in 1660 Archbishop William Juxon, who had accompanied Charles I to the scaffold, was raised to the See of Canterbury, and immediately set about repairing the ravages of the Cromwellians notably by rebuilding the Great Hall.

The private apartments are the most recent additions to the building, having been added by Edward Blore (d. 1879) for Archbishop Howley at the beginning of the 19th century. They overlook one of the loveliest gardens in London, a pleasance which has existed since the earliest occupation of the Palace.

Lambeth Palace is not only the Archbishop of Canterbury's official London residence, it also provides the venue for the Lambeth Conference of Anglican Bishops under the Archbishop's Presidency. This 'Lambeth Conference' as it is called was instituted in 1867 and is held every 10 years with more than 300 representatives from the United Kingdom, the Commonwealth and the United States.

The Tate Gallery, Millbank, Westminster.
Built in 1897, the Tate Gallery was
presented to the nation by Sir Henry Tate
(d. 1899), the sugar refiner and co-founder
of Tate & Lyle, to house a permanent
collection of British art. The original idea for
such a national collection had first been
mooted by Sir Francis Chantrey, the
sculptor, who in 1841 bequeathed his not
inconsiderable fortune to the Royal
Academy for the purpose.

The Collection includes works of art by
British artists from the Elizabethan age to
the present day, but it is particularly rich in
19th century paintings as it includes the
huge Turner bequest of nearly 300
canvasses. Turner, on his death in 1851,
left instructions in his will that the contents
of his studio, the oil-paintings and some
19,000 drawings now in the British
Museum were to be exhibited in a special
gallery to be built by the trustees of the
National Gallery with funds left by him for
the purpose. His wishes were never carried
out and the paintings came to the Tate
Gallery when, in 1910, Sir Joseph Duveen
had a special gallery built for them.

The Gallery also has a continual programme of loan exhibitions of British artists
of past centuries and modern artists from all
over the world. Many of its associated
activities have earned it the reputation of
being among the liveliest — and sometimes
the most controversial — on the London art
30   gallery scene.

Westminster Abbey, Parliament Square, Westminster. This was the site in Saxon times of a Benedictine abbey known as the 'West Monastery' (that is west of the city) hence the name 'Westminster'. Edward the Confessor — the last effective Saxon king — rebuilt the abbey and re-founded the Collegiate Church of St Peter in 1065AD. Edward himself was canonised in 1163 and in 1245 Henry III decided to rebuild the church on a magnificent scale to house the reliquary of the saint's remains. In 1298 a disastrous fire swept through the Abbey buildings destroying the infirmary, dormitory, refectory and cloister. A new cloister was built in 1365, but little more work was done on the church. The nave itself was left

unroofed until 1376 when it was rebuilt, the work being completed in 1388. The chantry for Henry V (1413-1422) was added in 1441. The next major addition was Henry VII's chapel built in 1509. The twin west towers with the gable between them were added by Nicholas Hawksmoor, a pupil of Wren, in 1739. Wren himself began renewing stonework in 1688 and repair work has been almost continuous since then.

The Abbey has a long royal connection, almost all the monarchs from William the Conqueror to Elizabeth II were crowned here and until the 19th century many of them were also buried here. One of the most outstanding tombs is that of Queen

Eleanor, beloved wife of Edward I (1272-1307), who died while he was fighting in Scotland. Her body was brought back from Harky in Nottinghamshire to London for burial, and at each place where the cortege rested at night, a stone cross was put up, the last of them being Charing Cross. Another is that of the murdered Richard II (1377-99) and his first Queen, Anne of Bohemia (d. 1394) with touching effigies of the tragic pair lying hand-in-hand. The effigies of Henry VII (1485-1509) and Elizabeth of York are the work of the Florentine sculptor, Pietro Torrigiani, they are of great beauty and undoubtedly the outstanding work of their date in England.

Westminster School, Dean's Yard, Westminster. Queen Elizabeth founded Westminster School in 1560 but there had been a monastic school on the site mentioned in the 14th century but it had been dissolved with the monastery in 1540, and initially the school used the former monastic buildings. The boys' schoolroom, where all the pupils were taught together until the end of the 19th century, was the former monks' dormitory, with a magnificent hammer beam roof. This was one of the tragic losses from the bombing in the last war. Like Winchester and Eton, Westminster was established with provision for 40 scholars whose fees were paid from a royal bursary, hence their title at Westminster of 'Queen's scholars'.

The school buildings are grouped around an irregular paved court called Little Dean's Yard. On the north side stands Ashburnham House, built for the Earls of Ashburnham in the middle of the 17th century, probably by John Webb (d. 1672), a pupil of Inigo Jones. The quality of carving, in particular on the staircase, is so high as to resemble the work of the master. The house, now used as the school library is open to the public during the Easter holidays. The stone gateway on the east side is part of Lord Burlington's additions of circa 1734. Only this and the facade of his building overlooking College Garden survived the bombing. All behind it had to be rebuilt.

The Victoria Tower of the Houses of Parliament is in the background.

Westminster Cathedral, Victoria Street, Westminster. When in the early 1970s the west side of Victoria Street was comprehensively redeveloped an opportunity arose for opening a piazza in front of the little known facade of the Roman Catholic Cathedral which was commissioned in 1910. The gay pink and white stripes of the brick and stone, the tympanum mosaic above the entrance and the enormous campanile now do a great deal to cheer up the rather dreary landscape of Victoria Street.

Both the architect John Francis Bentley and the Cathedral's initiator Cardinal Henry Vaughan, 3rd Archbishop of Westminster (d. 1903) chose a model taken from the early church and specifically the Hagia Sophia in Istanbul. This choice arose not only from a desire to avoid attempting to rival Westminster Abbey, scarcely a quarter of a mile away, but also for reasons of economy. Inside, glittering mosaics were designed to cover every surface, but above the gallery level there is still bare brick, as the money ran out before completion. In some of the side chapels one gets an idea of how the completed church would have looked and what has been lost through lack of funds.

The Campanile is an outstanding London landmark and viewpoint. It is open to the public — and has a lift.

Houses of Parliament, Westminster. Called the New Palace of Westminster, the Houses of Parliament are the seat of the supreme legislature of the United Kingdom and Northern Ireland and buildings on this site have been used for that purpose since 1547.

Early in the 11th century before the Norman conquest the Saxon king, Edward the Confessor (1042-66), moved court from Winchester to a building on this site. William Rufus, William the Conqueror's son added Westminster Hall in 1097-9. Miraculously it has survived all the turmoil and trouble of the intervening centuries. In particular it escaped the fire of 1834 when all else except the cloisters and the 18th century Law Courts were destroyed. In Westminster Hall various kings were brought to heel by their Commons: Edward II in 1327 and Richard II in 1399 were both forced to abdicate, Charles I was condemned to death in 1649. Commoners too, from Perkin Warbeck to Warren Hastings, were tried in the Hall. Monarchs and statesmen have lain in State here, the most recent being Sir Winston Churchill in 1965.

Each year in the second week of November, the monarch formally opens Parliament, and has done so for centuries. It was at James I's State Opening in 1605 that Guy Fawkes and his Catholic conspirators attempted to blow up the king and the Lords and Commons by setting light to barrels of gun powder hidden in the crypt under Westminster Hall.

The 'New Palace' is 19th century. In June 1835, following the devastating fire, a competition was announced to rebuild the Houses of Parliament on the same site and in the Gothic or Elizabethan style. The competition was won by Charles Barry (d. 1860), though much of the inventive detail was the work of A. W. N. Pugin (d. 1852) who, in the role of superintendent of wood carving, designed every detail from the stained glass, metal work and tiles, down to the coat-hangers and ink-stands. The House of Commons was destroyed by German bombs on 10 May 1941 but rebuilt in 1948-50 in keeping with Barry's work.

No 10 Downing Street, Westminster. Until the second half of the 17th century this site was occupied by the royal Cockpit, an annex of the old Tudor Palace of Whitehall. The house itself was built by Sir George Downing (d. 1684), a Harvard graduate who became secretary to the Treasury. It was granted by George II (1727-60) to Sir Robert Walpole (d. 1745), who accepted it as the official residence for the first Lord of the Treasury. Many of the succeeding occupants were Chancellors of the Exchequer. William Pitt the Younger is the longest recorded occupant of the house, living here from 1783-1803 with only one break of three years. He was simultaneously First Lord of the Treasury and Chancellor of the Exchequer. Benjamin Disraeli (d. 1881) made the house the official residence of the Prime Minister when he moved in during his last administration and so it has remained.

In 1806 No 11 Downing Street became the official residence of the Chancellor of the Exchequer and the two houses are joined inside. Architecturally the house has had only two main rearrangements since it was first built, when Sir Robert Walpole called in William Kent, many of whose interiors have survived. The second was in 1825 when Sir John Soane (d. 1837) remodelled the State Dining room, which rises through two floors. (In contrast he also designed the small private breakfast room.) The Cabinet Room — the heart of Government — is on the ground floor of No 10.

40

Horse Guards, Whitehall, Westminster. Another building close to the site of Henry VIII's Whitehall Palace — the guard house was here — is Horse Guards with its distinctive clock tower and bell. It is the headquarters of the Household Cavalry.

The present building was designed by William Kent (1685-1748), a protege of Lord Burlington, but it was not begun until 1750 after his death. Its Venetian windows and heavy quoining show the Palladian influence. Through the arch lies the Horse Guards Parade, where each year on the Queen's official birthday — usually in early June — the ceremony of the Trooping of the Colour is performed by the Guard's Division and the Household Cavalry. The Household Cavalry have their home in Knightsbridge Barracks but each day at 11am (10am on Sundays), dressed in their distinctive scarlet tunics with gleaming breast plates and plumed helmets they change guard in the small courtyard off Whitehall. Two mounted troopers are posted daily from 10am to 4pm and are relieved every hour. Two other troopers stand guard in the gateway itself.

The Banqueting House, Whitehall, Westminster. This magnificent example of classical architecture is all that survives of the former Whitehall Palace. It was built by Inigo Jones (d. 1652) for King James I (1603-25) and completed in 1622. Inigo Jones was primarily a stage designer working on the complicated sets for plays by Ben Jonson but in 1613 an opportunity arose for him to go to France and Italy in the train of the Duke of Arundel. Here he saw and studied the buildings of Palladio which were to have such an influence on English architecture throughout the 17th and 18th centuries. On his return to England he succeeded to the position of Surveyor General and during his surveyorship James I commissioned a total of three major works from him, of which the Banqueting Hall probably comes closest to a Palladian building.

The greatest glory is reserved for the interior. Charles I commissioned Peter Paul Rubens to paint nine allegorical ceiling paintings in panels depicting an apotheosis of James I and the joys brought by peace as a result of the unification of Scotland and England under the Stuart kings. Alas, this glorious peace was all too soon to be shattered by the Civil War and Charles I himself was beheaded in front of this very building on 30 January 1649.

The Banqueting Hall was fully restored in 1973 and is open to the public daily.

St James's Park, Westminster. Once a marshy meadow, St James's Park was drained by Henry VIII to adjoin his new Palace of St James's and converted into a deer park. Under the early Stuarts it became the favourite rendezvous for the Court and after his restoration in 1660 Charles II had it landscaped by the French designer Le Lotre with formal canals and cascades. It was remodelled by Nash for George IV in 1829 and the lake was added. Its popularity endured until the extra attractions of Vauxhall and Ranelagh relegated it to the nursery pleasures of perambulators and hoops. Now it serves an enormous office community with summer picnic places and winter walks along the edge of the water where many exotic birds, cranes and pelicans among them, disport themselves amongst the indigenous bird population.

46

Carlton House Terrace, The Mall, Westminster. This palatial row of terraced houses is an example of speculative building on a grand scale. When George IV decided in 1824 that living in the then Carlton House (pulled down in 1826) was 'little better than living in the street' he turned his attentions to improving Buckingham Palace. The cost of these improvements was scandalous and Parliament refused to countenance them. Partly to offset them, the Prince Regent casually granted John Nash leave to build on the site of Carlton House.

The terraces were constructed on earth dug from St James's Park when the new lake was created. Seen from the Park they form an impressive prospect, but the most brilliant part of the whole scheme, the Duke of York steps (on the extreme right) was not part of Nash's original concept. Indeed they were added in the teeth of his opposition. The column and statue to the Duke of York (seen here) were added even later — in 1833 — by Benjamin Wyatt (d. 1855).

The original intention was to sell apartments in these terraces to private people but most are now used for government or public offices. Many well known institutions have their headquarters in the terrace including the world famed Royal Society, founded in 1600. Among others are the Institute of Contemporary Arts, the Royal Society of British Artists and the Civic Trust.

48

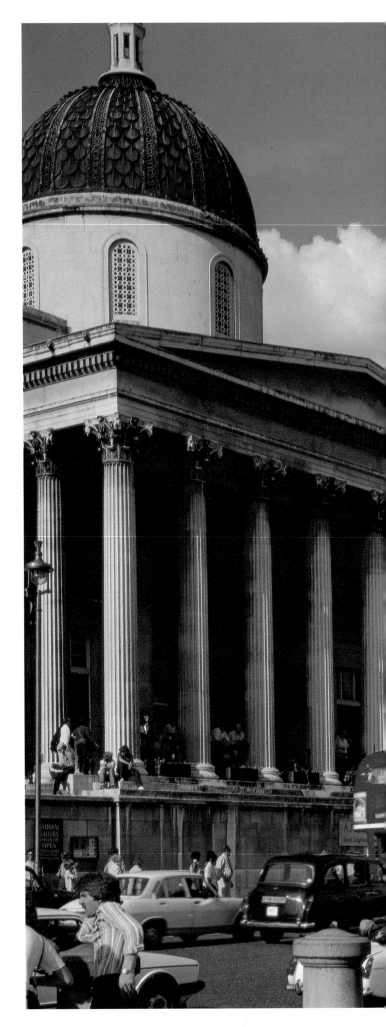

Trafalgar Square, Westminster. The concept of creating a grand 'circus' at the point where the north-south axis of Charing Cross road and Whitehall met the east-west axis of The Strand and The Mall came from John Nash who hoped to plan London on the model of Bath. The 'Square' itself was actually laid out in 1829-41 by Sir Charles Barry in commemoration of Nelson's great victory of 1805.

It provides a spectacular position for James Gibbs' church of St Martin-in-the-Fields seen here on the right. Built from 1722-6 the church's innovative west front combination of steeple with Corinthian portico has become a prototype for innumerable churches both in the United Kingdom and in Ireland and North America. Gibbs was a follower of Sir Christopher Wren and worked with him on several churches in London.

The focal point of the Square was supposed to be provided by the National Gallery on the north side but even the sloping site cannot give this building with its inadequate dome the necessary importance. The porticoes to left and right of the central block re-used the columns from the front of the Prince Regent's demolished Carlton House. The gallery designed by William Wilkins (1778-1839) was built in 1834-37 to house the collection of John Julius Angerstein and other publicly-owned collections, which it had been decided should be separated from the British Musuem. It contains an outstanding national collection, particularly rich in paintings of the early Italian, Venetian and Flemish schools.

The Square, as befits its public nature, is the repository of various monuments, principally Nelson's column, which stands 170ft high and was erected in 1839. The lions at its base are by Sir Edwin Landseer and were added in 1858. On the south side of the square there is a fine equestrian statue of Charles I by Le Sueur cast in 1633.

An enormous Christmas tree, a gift from the people of Norway, is placed in Trafalgar Square every year and many a New Year's revel ends with an icy bathe in the fountains.

The Royal Opera Arcade, Pall Mall, Westminster. One of the most delightful of the hidden corners of London, the Royal Opera Arcade is the oldest arcade in London but probably the least known. It runs from Pall Mall to Charles Street off St James's Square. The original shop fronts and ironwork lanterns and gates at either end, give it an architectural distinction superior to that of the Burlington or Piccadilly Arcades. It was designed by John Nash and G. S. Repton and built in 1816-1818 as part of a theatre now demolished. The proximity of New Zealand House on the corner has influenced some of the shop tenancies. Here, for example, is the New Zealand bookshop, a print shop selling the largest selection of topographical views of New Zealand available in London, rubbing shoulders with the Bank of New Zealand, not to mention the half dozen travel agents selling cheap flights to the Antipodes. But London re-asserts itself with a gunsmith's and several bespoke tailors and bootmakers.

Burlington House, Piccadilly, Westminster.
Old Burlington House was the London property inherited by the gifted third Earl of Burlington, architect and patron of the arts, in 1704 at the tender age of 10. Returning from the 'Grand Tour' in 1716, he set about transforming it in the light of the buildings he had seen by Palladio in Italy. He made it 'The only town residence really fit for a British nobleman' and beneath the heavy attic storey with niches containing statues of the great artists and architects of history and behind the ground floor colonnade a certain amount of Burlington's house remains. Particularly fine in design and ornament are rooms on the first floor overlooking the courtyard.

In 1854 Burlington House was acquired by the government to house, in the wings various learned societies — the Society of Antiquaries founded in 1707, is an example — and in the central block, the Royal Academy of Arts. The Academy has a continuous programme of exhibitions, including the renowned Summer Exhibition of paintings and sculpture by living professionals and amateurs which has been held since 1769. The post of President of the Royal Academy was first held by Sir Joshua Reynolds (d. 1792) whose statue stands in the courtyard in front of the Academy.

Piccadilly Circus, Westminster. At night, lit by up by garish neon signs, Piccadilly Circus is unlike any other area in this sometimes rather solidly well-behaved capital. It is the centre of theatreland, the 'West End' which is to London what Broadway is to New York. The oldest surviving London theatre is the Theatre Royal, Drury Lane, founded in the 17th century with the list of owner-managers sounding like a roll of honour of the entire English theatre: Garrick and Sheridan are examples. The great era of theatre-building was at the turn of the last century, an opulent period, and the interiors of many of them are often wonderfully gaudy with marble staircases, plaster putti and much gilt and plush.

'Eros', the statue which stands roughly at the centre of the triangular 'Circus', was put up in memory of the philanthropist peer Lord Shaftesbury (d. 1885), but it has now become so bound up in the mythology of London and so much its mascot that neither its creator, Alfred Gilbert, nor its dedication are readily remembered.

Liberty's, Regent Street, Westminster.
Liberty's is known throughout the world for
its printed silks and cottons, to which it has
given its name. The front facing Regent
Street is neo-classical stone grandeur at its
best, to fit in with the rest of Nash's
triumphal route from Carlton House Terrace
to Regent's Park, but round the corner, in
Great Marlborough Street one is suddenly
in fantasy land. Here is a genuine, purpose-
built, timber-framed department store, the
timbers are all functional and not merely
applied decoration, the windows are all
leaded and the roof tiles are all hand-made.
This is not just a facade. The swing doors,
which have linen fold panels, lead into a
fascinating interior where fashion is displayed amidst medieval mouldings and
carvings and grotesque animals peer out at
one from the banisters of the staircase. It
might have been built in 1524; in fact it was
built in 1924.

Cumberland Terrace, Regent's Park, Westminster. As early as 1793 John Fordyce, Surveyor General of Land Revenue had persuaded the Treasury to authorise a competition for designs to develop a Crown property known as Marylebone Park. Architects fought shy of the scheme until John Nash, a great impresario though previously only known for some country houses, submitted his plans in 1810. The scheme was revolutionary. For the first time in a major London development the grid pattern was abandoned in favour of a landscaped design resembling houses in a country park. Originally the scheme had entailed a number of villas in what is now the Inner Circle but these were omitted to allow for noble vistas through the Park. All the terraces went up in a great hurry between 1821-26, which explains the many accusations of jerry-building which have since been levelled at Nash.

The whole plan was intimately related to Nash's plan for remodelling the centre of London. The double York Terrace, the first to be reached from this south-east approach, only had access from the mews behind so that the palatial facade should suffer no interruption from doors. The finest terraces are probably Chester and Cumberland. Cumberland Terrace is the longest of all and has the most splendid Ionic portico surmounted by a pediment richly ornamented with terracotta sculptures in the antique taste which similarly decorate the balustrade of the two projecting end pavillions. The terrace has recently been most beautifully restored from the parlous state into which it had fallen after the last war.

60

The London Zoo, Regent's Park, Westminster. Officially 'The Gardens of the Zoological Society of London', London Zoo as it is better known was founded in 1828 by Sir Thomas Stamford Bingley Raffles, a famous naturalist and Lieutenant Governor of Java, who acquired Singapore for the British in 1819 where the world renowned hotel is named after him. The London Zoo was started as a scientific Zoological Society and it is here that its first duties still lie — studying animals and, where possible, breeding from them and in particular from endangered species. But it is as an entertainment that the Zoo is best known and loved by Londoners and visitors alike. The original five acres granted by Regent's Park to the Society grew as more and more animals arrived and better habitats were created for them. The most spectacular recent additions have been the Charles Clore house for small mammals, where nocturnal animals can be observed by 'night-light', Lord Snowdon's controversial aviary and the beautifully landscaped 'Great Cat' enclosures where tigers and lions can roam almost as in the wild, to the greater enjoyment of both themselves and the visitor. Seen here is, obviously, the Giraffe House. The Zoological Society is a self-financing charity which receives most of its funds from the gate-money. The Zoo is open daily, on the first Saturday of the month at a reduced rate.

The Post Office Tower seen from Fitzroy Square, Camden. This elegant square was begun in the 18th century, the south and east sides built by Robert Adam and the north and west sides were added in 1825 to complete the square.

Fitzroy Square has a long and distinguished literary history as a rash of blue plaques testify. No 29 was the home of the great Irish playwright, George Bernard Shaw, who lived here from 1887 until his marriage in 1898, and later of Virginia Woolf who set up home here with her brother in 1907-1911. Their regular Thursday evening gatherings of *literati* gave the celebrated 'Bloomsbury Group' its special identity.

The Post Office Tower, seen in the background, typifies communications in the 20th century. It was opened in 1965. It stands 580ft (177m) high with a 40ft radar aerial mast making it the tallest building in the country.

Kenwood House, Hampstead. Just off the road between Highgate and Hampstead, the twin hill-top villages overlooking London, stands Kenwood House. Now owned by the Greater London Council and housing the permanent collection of the Iveagh Bequest, it is open daily to the public. In summer the long sloping lawn in front of the house provides an admirable setting for theatrical and musical events and the adjacent Hampstead Heath provides a unique place of recreation for the whole of north London. It was here that Constable studied cloud effects and Keats heard the nightingale sing, for Hampstead, this fashionable suburb, has been the home of countless artists and writers as the plethora of blue plaques on many of its delightful Georgian houses will testify.

Kenwood House was, in 1766, a comparatively modest country house belonging to Lord Mansfield, then Lord Chief Justice, who employed Robert Adam to enlarge it. The principal additions were the Orangery in the west and the library to the east. The latter has one of the prettiest surviving Adam interiors. The Iveagh bequest contains many important paintings of the Dutch and English schools, outstanding amongst them a Rembrandt self-portrait, a Cuyp *View of the Dordecht*, a Vermeer interior, as well as portraits by Gainsborough and Reynolds.

St Pancras Station, Euston Road, Camden.
This celebrated 'Midland Region' station
was originally the London terminus of the
Midland Railway which early in its history
had an agreement with the Great Northern
to use Kings Cross. By the early 1860s
however the lines had become so con-
gested that the Midland decided to end the
agreement and build its own London
station. St Pancras went up remarkably
quickly and on 1 October 1868 the 4.15am
up mail from Leeds had the distinction of
being the first train to arrive at the station.
The railway line had to cross the Regent's
Canal on its way into St Pancras, and to
avoid unnecessarily steep gradients the
station platforms were raised between 15
and 17ft above street level. This gave the
station buildings great grandeur of height
and the vacant ground level space was used
to store barrels of ale from Burton-on-Trent,
one of the places served by the Midland.
The architect, W. H. Barlow, performed a
great feat of engineering in the impressive
vault over the platforms comprising a single
arch with a span of 245ft 6in, 100ft high
and 700ft long. It was the widest span at
that time in England. No London station in
those days was complete without a hotel,
and St Pancras was no exception. A competition was announced and won by Sir
George Gilbert Scott with his design rich in
14th century French and Italian Gothic
ornamentation. A major consideration with
the railway must have been a desire to out-
do their erstwhile hosts. The St Pancras
Hotel was to be bigger and grander than
any other, but almost all its wonderful
mosaic flooring and painted wall decora-
tions, beautiful wrought ironwork and rich
plaster ceilings were lost when in the
1930s the hotel was closed and the building converted to office use. Perhaps Scott
was right when he modestly claimed that it
68   was 'Possibly too good for its purpose'.

The British Museum, Great Russell Street, Holborn. Sir Hans Sloane left his collections of anthropological and natural history specimens to the nation on his death in 1753 and from 1759 onwards they were displayed to the public in Montague House in Bloomsbury. In the early 19th century three important collections of antique sculpture, including the famous Elgin Marbles, were acquired to form a national collection of antiquities. The acquisition of George III's library in 1823 and Mr Angerstein's pictures in the following year (later to form the nucleus of the National Gallery) made the building of a new and bigger museum imperative. The architect chosen was Sir Robert Smirke (d. 1867), whose grand design with the famous colonnade of Ionic columns is perhaps the grandest neo-Classical temple to the arts in London. Behind the colonnade there was an open court which was taken over by the library in 1852 and filled by the famous circular reading room with radiating desks beneath a great saucer dome. The principal collections of the Museum are still the antiquities — including the now controversial Elgin Marbles — books, manuscripts and drawings, but the anthropological collections are now in a separate 'Museum of Mankind' in Burlington Gardens, behind the Royal Academy.

Covent Garden, Westminster. Covent Garden takes its name from having been the kitchen garden of Westminster Abbey. In the early-17th century the fourth Earl of Bedford, then the landlord, commissioned Inigo Jones to design for him a piazza in the Italian or French mode as a select residential centre. The houses occupied two sides with an open arcade at street level, the Church of St Paul's, also by Inigo Jones the third side and Bedford House the fourth. All this, save the church, has now gone. In 1670 the Duke of Bedford obtained a royal charter to hold a market in the square and by the end of the century the market had become so large and successful as to be a nuisance to the residents. Fashionable tenants moved out leaving the buildings to shopkeepers. In 1828 the central open space was filled with the elegant Market Building of Charles Fowler (d. 1867). The central block, whose Tuscan portico echoes that of the church opposite, contains the original Regency shop fronts. By 1877 all the 17th century houses of the 'Piazza' had disappeared.

The removal of the fruit and flower market in 1974 to its new home in Nine Elms, left not only Fowler's market vacant, but also innumerable fruit and vegetable shops around the piazza which owed their existence to the proximity of the market. The area has attracted many smart 'fashion boutiques' as well as restaurants, wine bars and art galleries. Though many may regret the passing of the market itself, all should rejoice in the charm of the market buildings, revealed once more as a result of the redevelopment of the area.

The National Theatre, Lambeth. Even by the early 1930s the South Bank was increasingly being seen as an overspill area to ease the appalling problems of traffic congestion in the West End. It was the forgotten quarter of central London promising wonderful building opportunities for 'brave new architects'. The war intervened and it was only in the late '40s that plans were finally drawn up for a South Bank arts centre, to include a concert hall and national theatre. The area was chosen to be the site of the Festival of Britain, and the first building completed was the Festival Hall, opened in 1951. The rest was left till later. The Festival of Britain was a huge success, and its situation south of the river, proved no impediment to the enormous crowds. The result was a greatly renewed interest in the South Bank arts centre. The Queen Elizabeth Hall, the National Film Theatre, the Hayward Gallery and an extension to the Festival Hall were all quickly planned. Dance alone was unrepresented; Sadler's Wells which had hoped to move south did not receive sufficient government funding.

The National Theatre Company was founded in 1962 under the joint directorship of Laurence Olivier and John Gielgud. They were both part of the planning committee of the New National Theatre building, the architect, chosen by interview not competition, was Denys Lasdun. Three theatres were planned. The largest, the 'Olivier' (1,100 seats) has an open stage; the second, the 'Lyttleton' (900 seats) has a traditional proscenium stage; and the smallest, the 'Cottesloe' (400 seats) is an experimental studio theatre. A large foyer, on several floors, provides space for pre-theatre entertainments like musical recitals and poetry readings. The bare concrete within contrasts vividly with the traditional gilt and plush of most 'West End' theatres.

The York House Watergate, Victoria Embankment Gardens, Westminster. Just on the right as you emerge from the Embankment underground station is the Embankment Gardens, part of a narrow strip of gardens stretching east as far as the Temple and formed on reclaimed land after the building of the embankment. Here stands this ravishing little building, a reminder of how the river had once been the most comfortable and speediest route for Londoners to take when travelling about the city. The Gate, which gave access to the gardens of the Archbishop of York's house in the Strand, was erected in 1626, by Nicholas Stone (d. 1647). Though more a sculptor than an architect he had worked closely with Inigo Jones, which probably gave him the working knowledge to build such a confidently classical building with its heavy rustication, banded columns and big broken segmental pediment. The couchant lions and richly carved cartouche show the sculptor's hand. The whole is suitably ornamented with shells but the effect is somewhat lost when viewed across a municipal park rather than from the river as was intended.

76

The Royal Courts of Justice, The Strand, Westminster. As early as 1841 there had been demands from the newly-formed Law Society for the many non-criminal courts, dotted about London, to be placed under one roof. A site to the north of the Strand was chosen, it comprised seven and three quarter acres of slums then known as Carey Street — the name which has entered the language as synonymous with bankruptcy. It was not until 1868, after a competition contested by 11 architects, that a shambling committee gave the commission to G. E. Street, but with so many restrictions on cost and in the disposal of offices that, in his son's opinion, the business killed him. This son, Arthur E. Street, was entrusted with the completion of the building after his father's death in 1881.

As seen here, from the west, the Courts show a picturesque juxtaposition of turrets, gables and pinnacles building up to the great clock tower over the Central Hall. This great chamber was the principal feature of Street's design, a tremendous gothic extravaganza and it is fitting that beneath the huge stone vaulted ceiling should sit a memorial statue of the architect of this Victorian palace of justice, presented by the American Bar Association in 1924.

Somerset House, Victoria Embankment, Westminster. Before the building of the Embankment, the terrace in front of Somerset House overlooked the broad sweep of the Thames and not as it does today, a crowded, lorry-packed thoroughfare. This view was painted in 1750 by the Venetian artist Antonio Canaletto and his painting is now in the royal collection. The terrace stands on a rusticated basement colonnade and on the keystone of the river entrance arch in the centre appears the head of the river god, reminding us that once, as at Venice, this colonnade was washed by the teeming waters of the capital's waterway.

Somerset House was built in 1776 as public offices, an innovation at that date. Now the government offices, including the central record of births and deaths for which Somerset House was most famous in the middle of the 19th century, have now moved to new premises. The learned societies which once occupied the Strand front have moved too — to Burlington House, Piccadilly — though their names still appear over the entrance from the Strand. The Royal Academy Exhibition's rooms, the finest in the building, are still awaiting a permanent use.

Astor Estate Office, Temple Place, Westminster. William Waldorf Astor was an immensely rich American who fled to Britain in 1890 feeling that in this country at least his wealth could buy him all he could want — as he declared 'England is a country fit for a gentleman to live in'. Unfortunately England was somewhat slow to clasp him to its bosom. In the hopes of influencing opinions he purchased two outstanding literary and political newspapers of the day, the *Pall Mall Gazette* and the *Pall Mall Magazine*. To run this burgeoning newspaper empire he built for himself the Astor Estate Office, the most extraordinary private office building in London. It is built of Portland stone in an early-Elizabethan style. Inside, it boasts a staircase hall with a first floor gallery with ebony columns and a first floor 'Great Hall' with a hammer beam roof from where business was conducted.

Astor's adopted country did finally recognise him when he donated more than half a million pounds to various royal charities to alleviate the hardships of the wounded and the widows and orphans of fallen soldiers in World War 1. In 1916 he was raised to the peerage as Baron Astor of Hever. His daughter-in-law was the charismatic Nancy Astor who was the first woman Member of Parliament to take her seat and the subject of a celebrated television series.

82

Fishmongers' Hall, London Bridge Approach, City of London. The Fishmongers' Company is one of the 12 great livery companies of the old City of London, founded in the 13th century when much more fish was consumed and fortunes could be made by those who controlled the trade. Unlike most of the other medieval guilds, the Fishmongers do still retain some duties of trade control, and they also administer a school as well as other charities. Their hall has one of the best sites in London, the same one that it has occupied since the building of its first hall in 1504 on land belonging to a leading fishmonger. The present hall was built in 1834 after the destruction of the earlier building by the collapse of the adjacent London Bridge. The architect was Henry Roberts (d. 1876) who was most ably assisted by his young draughtsman, Gilbert Scott. The design required a tall basement storey to raise the building from the level of the river to that of the newly erected London Bridge. On the east facade appear the arms of the company with merman and mermaid supporters. Inside the arms appear again in several places with another fishy emblem, a dolphin, cavorting on overdoors, and furniture and, most impressively, on the Company's ancient silver and gold plate.

Holborn Viaduct, City of London. Holborn Viaduct was built in 1863-9 as a much needed improvement to the communications of the City with the West End. It bridges the steep valley 'Hole Bourne', the upper part of the Fleet river, one of London's many underground rivers, which by the middle of the 18th century had become little better than an open sewer. Public outcry led to its being covered over in 1765. The viaduct stretches for almost a quarter of a mile and cost the City ratepayers £2½million. The architect was Joseph Cubitt.

The jolly irón balustrade has recently been painted a glowing laquer red and everywhere the City's griffins cavort. Upon the bridge are four bronze statues representing the Victorian demi-gods of 'Commerce', 'Science', the 'Fine Arts' and 'Agriculture'.

The Central Criminal Court, City of London.
Popularly known as the 'Old Bailey' after the
street on which it fronts, the Central
Criminal Court was built from 1900-7 on
the site of the notorious Newgate Prison,
demolished in 1902. There is a fine Baroque
feel to the rusticated basement and the
windows with their heavy Gibbs surrounds.
The copper dome was inspired by the
domes of Greenwich. It is surmounted by a
gilt statue of 'Justice' — blindfolded with
sword and scales. The building has been
extended since the war.

Newgate was London's principal prison
from the 13th century onwards. It was
rebuilt in 1770 but, only 10 years later, it
was set on fire during the Gordon riots. Lord
George Gordon, the organiser of the anti-
Catholic riots, died in Newgate of gaol fever
in 1793. The appalling conditions in this
prison were a national scandal and of major
concern to the great prison reformer,
Elizabeth Fry (d. 1845), so it is fitting that a
statue of her should stand in the main hall
of the Old Bailey. On the first two days of
each session the judge carries a nosegay
and sweet herbs are spread about the
Court, a survival from the days when the
noxious smells of the neighbouring prison
might have suffocated the court. During
hearings the visitors' gallery is open to the
public.

Smithfield Market, City of London. It is hard to imagine amidst the roar of the lorries that this was once the 'Smoothfield' without the city walls where, in medieval times, jousts and tournaments were held. It was also the site of the St Bartholomew Fair, the most important cloth fair in England in the middle ages. More sinisterly it was a place of execution. In the 16th century it was the site of the hideous fires when some 270 Protestants under Queen Mary were martyred and, only a few years later, where many Catholics met a similar fate under Queen Elizabeth I.

But even before these infamous events it was a meat and cattle market as which it is still famous. Smithfield is the sole remaining market of the three which had served the capital since Elizabethan times. Covent Garden, the fruit, flower and vegetable market has crossed the river to a new site at Nine Elms and Billingsgate, the fish market, has recently moved down river to West India Dock.

90

Cloth Fair, St Bartholomew-the-Great, City of London. A narrow street running down beside the ancient church of St Bartholomew-the-Great, Cloth Fair, was once a fashionable part of London. The fine house on the corner (No 41) with wooden oriel windows dates from the 17th century and one of a few that survived the Great Fire of 1666. In medieval times, when the St Bartholomew's Fair was a great annual festival, the famous court of 'Pie Powder' (a corruption of *pied poudre*) was held in Cloth Fair. At this court weights and measures of the goods on sale were tested. The name was given to the court because justice was meted out there as speedily 'as dust falls from the foot'.

When at the end of the 17th century following the Fire fashionable London began to move west, this area was allowed to fall into decrepitude. Houses became warehouses and tenements and it is only recently when it came under threat of redevelopment that any serious interest was paid to this ancient street. The name still has significance — at least one specialist shop sells nothing but felts and baize.

The Entrance Gateway, St Bartholomew-the-Great, West Smithfield, City of London. Away from the roar and bustle of Smithfield stands St Bartholomew-the-Great, one of the very few remaining Norman churches in London. Though most of it has been rebuilt, a good deal of the original remains, including the delightful gateway from West Smithfield seen here. The gateway itself is of stone and was carved in the 13th century. The timber-framed house above it is Elizabethan and built about 1595. Its presence was revealed in 1915 when a bomb from a German Zeppelin blew away its tiled facade. The stone arch was originally the

entrance to an Augustinian priory, founded in 1123 with its adjoining hospital. St Bartholomew's Hospital, though totally rebuilt in the 18th century, is the oldest hospital foundation in London and still one of the most respected medical schools in the country. Inside the church the earliest part is the chancel, with great circular piers supporting round headed arches ornamented with dog-tooth carving in the Norman style. Small windows set high up in the clerestory dimly light this venerable church which retains a national reputation for its music.

The Barbican, London Wall, City of London. The Barbican development scheme was planned in the late 1950s with the idea of injecting some cultural life into the City of London which tended to be deserted after 5.30pm. The name is taken from the old city walls, once defensible, the 'barbican' being the name used for the outer gatehouse of a fort — a Roman fort was found on the site when bomb damage was cleared in 1950. The scheme began with the erection of tower blocks of flats in 1963. The three main towers are 412ft high and were at the time of building the tallest residential blocks in Europe. Soon after their erection work started on the public buildings intended to be the new London art centre. The scheme now incorporates the Guildhall School of Music and Drama, the City of London School for Girls and provides new permanent homes for the London Symphony Orchestra and the Royal Shakespeare Company, the latter moving from the Aldwych only recently.

96

St Paul's Cathedral, Ludgate Hill, City of London. St Paul's Cathedral is the masterpiece of the greatest architectural genius England has ever produced, Sir Christopher Wren. Old St Paul's, the 13th century cathedral that formerly occupied this site, had fallen into considerable disrepair by the beginning of the 17th century and despite some rebuilding by Inigo Jones it was still in need of considerable work when, in 1666, the Great Fire of London consumed its whole fabric. Sir Christopher Wren, as Surveyor General of the Works under Charles II, had already been consulted about repairs and the Commissioners naturally turned to him for plans to rebuild it. During the next eight years Wren worked on no less than five complete plans and designs for the Cathedral while trying out some of the designs on the 46 churches destroyed by the fire for the rebuilding of which he was also responsible. During these years he gathered around him a brilliant team of craftsmen whose names reappear constantly — Nicholas Hawksmoor his Clerk of the Works; John Longland, master carpenter; Thomas and Edward Strong, masons; Henry Doogood, plasterer; and the most famous of all, Grinling Gibbons, wood carver; and Jean Tijou, ironworker. The first stone was laid in 1675 and the last one in 1710.

Wren saw in the aftermath of the Fire an opportunity of rebuilding a fair city with wide thoroughfares and fine piazzas. He had designed a piazza not unlike Inigo Jones' Covent Garden, to set off his new cathedral, but the Crown Commissioners had neither the will nor the foresight to build other than in the cramped fashion which existed before the Fire. Wren's masterpiece is in consequence glimpsed set high on Ludgate Hill, up flights of stairs, down narrow lanes or most fittingly across the river but never set off, as Wren had wished, by a great square. Furthermore, many of the prospects of the cathedral we enjoy today are due to the spaces cleared after the bombing of World War 2. St Paul's then survived the second fire of London, not unscathed, but sustaining damage that was repairable.

St Paul's Cathedral — the High Altar. One of Sir Christopher Wren's early designs had been for a church with a plan based on an equal-armed Greek cross but this did not fulfil the church's liturgical requirements, so, somewhat against his will, he extended the nave to make a traditional Latin longitudinal cross, but here all is light and space, so different from some of the medieval cathedrals. The choir stalls and organ are the work of Grinling Gibbons and the great gilded gates are by Jean Tijou, who made wrought iron as delicate as lace. Though building work continued for more than 35 years, the cathedral was first used on 2 December 1697 when a service of thanksgiving was offered for the Peace of Ryswick.

St Paul's contains the monuments of many warrior heroes, amongst them Nelson, Wellington and Gordon but also a galaxy of painters, Van Dyck, Reynolds and Turner. But surely the most moving monument must be that of the great architect himself, who, in his 90th year, 1722, was carried on a litter to see his cathedral completed, though he himself had been dismissed ingominiously for slow progress in 1718 after 40 years of faithful service.

St Paul's is the parish church of the City of London and the seat of its bishop. As everywhere in the City, the Lord Mayor is pre-eminent, both he and the Lady Mayoress have their own boxes in the choir and when Prince Charles broke with tradition and was married here, rather than at Westminster Abbey, the Lord Mayor greeted the Sovereign at the great West door and escorted her down the nave.

The High Altar and its windows were damaged by a direct hit in 1941 and were replaced in 1958 to designs by W. Godfrey Allen and S. E. Dykes Bower. They serve as Britain's memorial to over 324,000 men and women of the Commonwealth who died in two world wars.

The Bank of England, Threadneedle Street, City of London. London remains the pre-eminent banking capital of the world. At the centre of this capital stands the Bank of England (seen here on the left of the photograph) with its hundreds of satellite banks crowding close around it.

A 'Bank of England' was first incorporated by Royal Charter in 1694 though its prime duty, financing the king, had been undertaken for many years before this by goldsmiths. The oldest part of the present building is the exterior wall with its blank arcade of Corinthian columns, the remains of Sir John Soane's great Bank of England begun in 1788. The rest is hidden and disguised under Sir Herbert Baker's monstrous additions between 1924 and 1939. Beneath, in the vaults, lie the nation's gold reserves, which, until 1973, were guarded nightly by a detachment of guards. Now despite modern electronic protection devices, one of the Bank's 16 directors has always to be on the premises both night and day.

Here at the very centre of the City of London lies the small square on which stands the Bank, the Mansion House, official residence of the Lord Mayor of London built 1739-53, the Royal Exchange the third to occupy this site and built 1842-44 (in the centre of the picture). As the inscription on the portico recalls, the first was built by Sir Thomas Gresham in 1565, the great financier who restored financial stability to Elizabethan England by stabilising the currency. It is now the home of the newly opened London International Financial Futures Exchange. The modern building behind the Bank and the Royal Exchange is the 26-storey Stock Exchange completed in 1970.

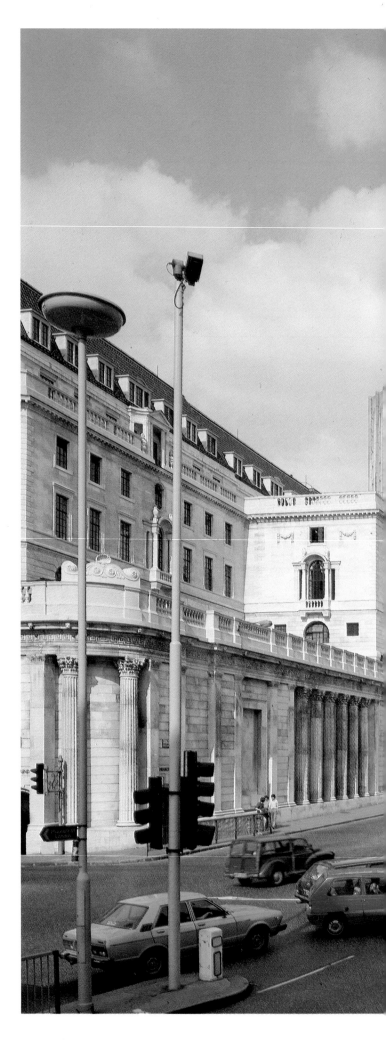

The Monument, Fish Street Hill, City of London. 'The Monument' was designed by Sir Christopher Wren in 1671 to com-memorate the Great Fire of London of 1666 and erected close to the site of the baker's shop in Pudding Lane where the fire broke out. Wren's first design was for a column spurting out tongues of flame reaching upwards to where a phoenix surmounted a flaming urn. This design was finally rejected on grounds of aesthetics, cost and safety — the latter because Wren considered the spread wings of the phoenix would be a danger in a strong wind. This simpler design was chosen instead and the fluted Doric column is surmounted by an urn with a gilt flaming ball. Originally a plaque at the base of the Monument bearing a Latin inscription stated that the fire had been caused *'by the treachery and malice of the Popish faction,'* a charge for which there were few grounds. It was removed in 1831.

The Monument is open daily and from the gallery, 200 feet up, there is a fine view over the City.

The Tower of London, Tower Hill, City of London. The earliest part of the building, the White Tower seen here, was begun by William the Conqueror in 1078 shortly after his arrival in London. The hasty building of this mighty fortress was to serve a dual purpose, first, to protect the city of London on the river side and second, to overawe any citizens planning an uprising against the Normans. In the succeeding 900 years of its history the Tower has served in turn as a citadel, royal palace, state prison and arsenal.

Another early building — founded in the 12th century but since rebuilt — is the Chapel Royal of St Peter ad Vincula (St Peter in Chains) which contains the graves and memorials of many of the people who were executed here. The historian Macaulay called it 'The saddest spot on earth'. The tower is surrounded by the Inner Ward, a massive wall surmounted by 13 towers and the Outer Ward with six towers facing the river. These defences were encircled by a wide moat, now dry.

Many kings sought refuge here in times of trouble and Henry I built a royal palace within the walls, which was subsequently demolished by Oliver Cromwell. One king died here, when in 1483, the little Princes, the young Edward V and the Duke of York were both murdered, possibly at the instigation of their uncle, the Duke of Gloucester, later Richard III. A medieval tradition was that all the kings and queens of England spent the night before their coronation in the Tower. In the morning they progressed to Westminster by river. Charles II was the last monarch to observe this custom although his procession to the coronation was through the streets of London.

The infamous 'Traitors Gate' is the river entrance by which prisoners arrived, brought by barge from trial in Westminster Hall. Among the many distinguished prisoners were two queens of Henry VIII, Anne Boleyn and Catherine Howard, and one of his most faithful servants, Sir Thomas More, all of whom were executed.

A major attraction for the thousands of visitors is the Crown Jewels, housed in a specially constructed strong room which was opened in 1967. Most of the present royal regalia post-dates the Commonwealth as much of the older collection was melted down for gold to pay the Parliamentarian troops. The collection includes two of the most famous diamonds in the world, the Koh-i-Nor, which was presented to Queen Victoria in 1850 and the Star of Africa, the largest cut diamond in the world.

The ship in the photograph is the brig *Inca*, 124 years old.

Tower Bridge, City of London. With its fairy tale Gothic profile, its pinnacles and its fluttering banners, Tower Bridge dwarfs and almost casts into shade its truly medieval neighbour, the Tower of London. It was completed between 1886-1894 and it is the last bridge on the Thames before the new barrier and the sea. Its twin bascules, as is evident here, were designed to be raised to allow tall ships to pass into the Pool but with dock closures the facility is rarely used nowadays. All the original machinery for raising and lowering the Bridge is still in use, though electric motors have replaced hydraulic engines. Pedestrians were intended to walk across the upper bridge, a dizzy 112ft above the water and recently after much restoration work, this upper walk has been opened again.

Greenwich Hospital, Greenwich. English monarchs had an interest in Greenwich from the 15th century and a royal palace, Placentia, was built here in 1428. James I gave the palace to his Queen, Anne of Denmark, and his daughters Mary and Elizabeth were born there, but she, wanting something smaller, commissioned Inigo Jones to built her what is known as the 'The Queen's House'. Charles II on his restoration in 1660 decided to replace the rambling Tudor building with a new one and work began in 1664. Part of this palace still remains as the King Charles block. In 1694 William and Mary gave Greenwich over to the Navy as a hospital for sick and pensioned sailors, the counterpart of Chelsea, preferring to live themselves in their new wing at Hampton Court. The architect for the new hospital was Sir Christopher Wren.

In the south-west block is the banqueting hall known as the 'Painted Hall' because of its painted ceiling by Thornhill depicting the apotheosis of the monarchs who had been benefactors of the hospital. Building work continued throughout the reigns of William and Mary, Queen Anne and George I and the interior of the chapel, in the south-east block seen here, was not finally completed until 1789.

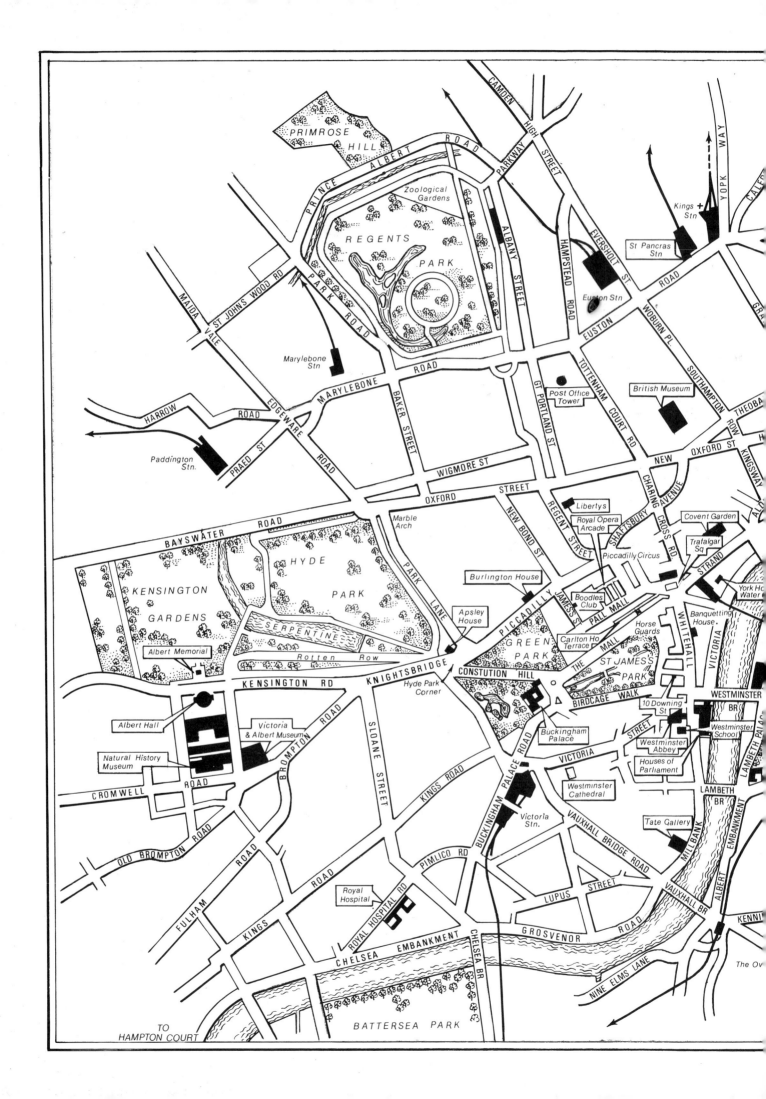